W9-CFC-413

TABLE OF CONTENTS

A long time ago, the bear had a long, shiny tail. He was very proud of his silky tail, which he waved for everyone to see — including the tricky fox.

One winter day, the fox decided to play a trick on the bear. Out on the frozen lake, the fox cut a hole. When the bear walked by, he saw many fat fish in a circle on the ice around the fox. Down in the fishing hole, the fox twitched his tail and pulled out another fat fish.

"Hello brother," said the fox. "How are you today?"

"Greetings brother," said the bear. "What are you doing?" he asked, as he looked at all the fat fish.

"I am fishing. Would you like to try?"

"Oh yes," said the bear. He could already taste the fat fish that he planned to catch.

"We will make a new hole for you, since I have already taken all the fish from this one," suggested the tricky fox. Then the fox led the big, bumbling bear to the shallow part of the lake where he knew very well that no fish could be found in the winter.

When the new hole was ready, the fox explained, "You must clear your mind of all thoughts of fish and concentrate. You must not even think too much or the fish will hear you. Turn your back and place your tail in the hole. Then when a fish grabs your tail, pull it out."

"But if my back is turned, how will I know when a fish bites?"

"I will hide over there where the fish cannot see. When I shout, pull as hard as you can, but do not move until then. You must be patient," said the fox.

"I will do exactly as you explained," whispered the bear as he sat down next to the hole. He placed his lovely long tail down into the icy cold water, turned his back, and waited.

It started to snow and the fox watched for a while, but then he went home to sleep in his cozy bed. The next morning, the fox woke up, thought about the bear, and went to check on him.

What a funny sight he found at the pond. There was the bear, looking like a small hill of snow, sleeping away in the exact spot where the fox had left him. He was snoring so loudly that the ice was shaking. The fox shook with laughter and then quietly crept up close to the bear's ear. Then he took a deep breath and shouted, "Now bear!"

The bear woke up startled and pulled with great force. When he pulled — swoosh — off went the part of his tail that was stuck solid in the ice. The bear turned around to see the fish he caught, but he was dismayed to see his beautiful, sleek tail frozen solid in the lake. The fox swiftly ran away as the angry bear chased him.

To this day, the bear has a short tail and no love for the fox. So, if you hear a bear moaning in the woods, remember that he may still be upset about his lost tail and how the fox tricked him.

What Did the Story Say?

Read > Write the answers.

1. What was the bear so proud of?

_____

2. How do the bear and the fox greet each other?

_____

3. Why did the fox take the bear to the shallow part of the lake?

_____

4. Besides placing his tail in the hole, what else did the fox tell the bear to do to catch a fish?

_____

5. What was causing the ice to shake?

_____

6. What was causing the fox to shake?

_____

7. Why do you think the bear listened to the fox?

_____

8. Why do you think the bear pulled so hard?

_____

9. What reasons does the bear have for moaning in the woods?

_____

How the Bear Lost his Tail
A Native American Tale

What Happened Next?

Read Number the sentences in the correct order to tell the story.

☐ The fox sat with a circle of fat fish around him.

☐ The fox decided to play a trick on the bear.

☐ The fox took the bear to the shallow part of the lake.

☐ The bear turned his back and stuck his tail in the fishing hole.

☐ The bear has no love for the fox.

☐ The fox went home to sleep in his cozy bed.

☐ The bear chased the swift fox.

☐ The fox shouted in the bear's ear.

☐ The bear lost the part of his tail that was stuck to the ice.

☐ The fox thought the bear looked like a small hill of snow.

Cathleen was stunned as she silently stared, afraid to even breathe. There he was, singing a sad little tune. He had pointy ears, a long, red beard, and the wrinkles of an old man. As he sang, he tapped a tiny hammer on a pair of shiny black shoes laid out on his leather apron.

Cathleen had waited for this moment for as far back as she could remember. She quickly recalled what her grandmother had told her: "Every leprechaun has a secret pot of gold. If you catch the leprechaun, the gold is yours — that is, if they don't trick you out of the prize!"

Determined to claim the pot of gold, she jumped out from behind the tree and shouted, "I see you, Mr. Leprechaun, so don't even move! I am much bigger, but I don't want to harm you."

The leprechaun threw down the hammer and jumped up. His face was red and he was shaking his tiny fist. "Oh, harm me you say? I think not! You were trying to frighten me to death. You're a fine tricky one, young miss."

"Put down your fist," Cathleen said firmly. "My grandmother warned me years ago how you will try to trick me out of my pot of gold. But I'm much too clever for that. Show me where it is at once! I'll follow you closely to make sure you don't try to sneak away."

The leprechaun lowered his fist and said, "Fine, just fine. I know your kind. The greedy are forever trying to rob us wee people of our treasures. What a shame to lose such a great pot of gold! Very well then, miss," he said with a wave of his hand.

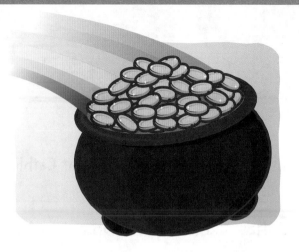

Cathleen followed the little fellow into the woods. The deeper they went, the darker it got — and the more difficult it was to see. But Cathleen was determined to keep her eye on the leprechaun, who she knew could vanish in an instant. If that happened, she would not get the gold.

Suddenly, the leprechaun stopped in front of a large tree. "Well now, I must do a bit of magic," he said.

With her eyes fixed upon him, Cathleen started to hear sounds in the woods. First she heard crickets, then the hoot of an owl, and then she heard the wind whistle through the trees. Finally, Cathleen heard a loud rustling in the leaves. It was so frightening that she could not stop herself from looking away from the leprechaun to see what was making the sound. When she did, she heard a shrill laugh as the leprechaun leapt away.

Cathleen jumped up and down in fury. She shouted, "Next time — and I know there will be one — you won't trick me!"

What Did the Story Say?

 Read Write the answers.

1. Describe the leprechaun that Cathleen saw.

_____

2. How did the leprechaun react when Cathleen surprised him?

_____

3. Who warned Cathleen about how a leprechaun can trick people?

_____

4. What does the leprechaun think about big people?

_____

5. Name three sounds Cathleen heard in the woods.

_____

_____

6. What mistake did Cathleen make that caused her to lose the pot of gold?

_____

_____

7. Do you think Cathleen will have better luck the next time? Why?

_____

_____

Word Meanings

 Read Write the word next to its meaning.

1. _____ remember

2. _____ smart

3. _____ man

4. _____ tiny

5. _____ crackling

6. _____ anger

7. _____ high-pitched

8. _____ disappear

shrill
fellow
fury
recall
clever
wee
rustling
vanish

Think About it!

 Read How would you spend a whole pot of gold?
Write your answer.

_____

_____

_____

Imagine that you are going on a long journey at sea. You have only some sketchy unfinished maps and no other information. As you are heading toward this strange new land, you have no idea what kinds of plants, animals, and people might live there. Are you scared? Excited? Thrilled?

For Captain James Cook of England, this was life. In the 1760s and 70s, Captain Cook traveled all over the world in search of new lands. Because of his excellent map-making skills, he was first chosen to travel to the Pacific. His government wanted to find out for sure if there was a continent in the far southern parts of the world. On this voyage, Captain Cook and his crew were the first people from Europe to travel along the east coast of Australia and throughout New Zealand. He claimed the new land for England and named it New South Wales.

Later, Cook traveled farther south than any other known explorer before him. He went as far south as the Antarctic Ocean and then around the entire globe in these waters. Before his historic adventures, lands in the southern oceans were often drawn very sketchy on maps, but his detailed notes and measurements helped correct these early maps.

Captain Cook discovered many islands and kept detailed notes about the people, their culture, and languages. He also proved there were no more continents to be found.

Because of his journeys, many improvements were made in the way crews prepared for long sea trips. Fewer sailors died on his explorations because of Captain Cook's belief in getting fresh foods at each stop. The fresh food helped to keep the whole crew healthier.

Captain Cook's travels allowed him to discover the Hawaiian Islands, which he named the Sandwich Islands. But Cook was not satisfied to remain in the southern waters, so he traveled the west coast of Canada and up through the coast of Alaska as well.

Even though he was very successful, Cook's journeys were not problem free. There were times when island people grew angry at his crews for taking too much food. Sometimes they were even attacked. In fact, in the end, Cook died during one of these attacks in the Hawaiian Islands.

Today, it is easy to find a map or a picture of just about any place in the world. But before TV, the Internet, and photography, people of the world relied on brave adventurers like Captain James Cook and his crewmen to tell them what was out there on this great big planet.

What Did the Story Say?

Read ▷ Circle the correct answer.

1. Captain James Cook was best know as a(n) _____.
   a. explorer
   b. cook
   c. musician

2. Captain Cook's crew were the first to travel the coast of _____.
   a. Africa and New Guinea
   b. Australia and New Zealand
   c. Austria and New Cumberland

3. Through his extensive travels, Captain Cook proved that all the _____ had been discovered.
   a. countries
   b. continents
   c. oceans

4. Fewer sailors died on Captain Cook's explorations because he believed in _____.
   a. making many stops
   b. giving them clean clothes
   c. feeding them fresh food

5. In his travels, Captain Cook discovered a group of islands he named the Sandwich Islands. These island were later renamed the _____.
   a. Hawaiian Islands
   b. Cook Islands
   c. New Zealand Islands

6. When islanders got angry with Captain Cook's crew, it was because they _____.
   a. bought too many souvenirs
   b. brought too many pets on shore
   c. took too much of the island food

Puzzle Fun

Read Use the clues to complete the puzzle.

1. James Cook's detailed notes helped to _____ some of the early map sketches.
2. James Cook traveled the world in _____ of new land.
3. James Cook was first recognized for having excellent _____ making skills.
4. James Cook was known in his day for travelling farther _____ than any other explorers.
5. James Cook went as far south as the _____ ocean.
6. James Cook is known for discovering the islands of _____, which are now part of the United States.
7. James Cook also visited what is now known as Australia and New Zealand, naming them _____ South Wales.

Read Use the shaded letters to complete the sentence.

James Cook was a very impressive sea _____ who made many discoveries in the mid 1700s.

"Not the balloon ride, Mom!" wailed Maddie as she looked longingly at the Ferris wheel. "For goodness sakes, it's the slowest ride at the carnival. It's even tied down."

"If you ride this with me, I guess I'll go on that with you later," her mom said nervously as she pointed to the Ferris wheel.

"It's a deal," said Maddie.

After a short wait in line they gave their tickets to the balloon ride operator. Then they climbed into the basket and stood next to the sandbags. The operator climbed in after them and started with an overview of how a hot air balloon works.

"In ballooning, this large basket is called the gondola. It is tied to the balloon, which is filled with hot air. The hotter the air, the higher the balloon will rise.

"The sandbags are the ballast, or extra weight, that the balloon carries," the operator continued. "If we want to rise quickly, we can throw them out to decrease the weight being lifted by the balloon. Today we will take a short ride straight up. I will heat the air inside the balloon using this gas-fired burner and we'll rise slowly. Don't worry, the gondola is tied securely to the ground."

Just as he was assuring the passengers that the balloon would not go up high, there was a strange, loud crackling sound. When he jumped out to check what was causing the sound, the anchor line snapped.

Maddie and her mom were shocked. They were too scared to move as the balloon rose up into the air. Soon they were looking down at a screaming crowd and it was too high to jump out.

"I think we're going to have to figure a way out of this mess, Maddie," said Mom, surprisingly calm. "I don't want to scare you, but we could be in serious trouble if we get near any trees or power lines."

Maddie's mind was racing as she thought about what could happen. She looked out over the edge only to see that they were headed straight for the Ferris wheel.

"Quick, Mom!" she shouted. "Fire up the burner. We need to rise up before we slam into that ride."

As her mom fired the burner, Maddie threw out the sandbags. They landed with a splash in the duck pond below. The two were working frantically when suddenly they heard cheering. The balloon had stopped drifting and they landed right on top of the Ferris wheel. Somehow the gondola got wedged between two seats.

"I told you I would ride the Ferris wheel with you, Maddie," Mom chuckled with relief. Then she gave Maddie a big hug.

What Did the Story Say?

 Read Fill in the blank to finish the sentence.

1. Maddie really wanted to ride on the _____.

2. The large basket attached to a hot air balloon is called the

   _____ .

3. There was a strange, loud _____ sound right
   before the balloon started drifting away.

4. A person can throw out the _____ to
   decrease the weight being lifted by the balloon.

5. Maddie's mom fired up the _____ to get
   the balloon to rise.

6. Maddie and her mom heard _____ when
   they landed on top of the Ferris wheel.

Think About it!

 Read At the end of the story, the characters land on top of the
Ferris wheel. How do you imagine they got down to the
ground? Write your answer.

_____

_____

_____

A Trip Around Your Neighborhood!

Read Write a short story about a balloon trip you would take over your neighborhood. Then draw a picture that goes with your story.

_____

_____

_____

_____

_____

_____

_____

_____

On a warm summer day in many parts of this country, ice can fall from the sky. Too strange you say? Well, this is true. The ice comes in the form of a hailstorm.

Like other types of precipitation, hail is a form of water that returns to the earth. In hailstorms, rain takes on a frozen round or lumpy shape, called a hailstone. These hailstones can be as small as peas or as large as baseballs. And, on rare occasions, they can be even larger. But most hailstones are smaller than 1 inch (2.5 centimeters) in diameter.

High up in the thunderclouds, hailstones start out as frozen raindrops or snow pellets called hail embryos. These embryos move on air currents and updrafts inside the hailstorm until they reach an area of hail growth. Here, the embryos collide with supercooled water droplets, which remain a liquid at temperatures well below the normal freezing temperature. The droplets freeze on the embryos causing them to grow into the larger hailstone.

There are several ways a hailstone can become large: (1) if it stays where there is a large amount of supercooled liquid water, (2) if the storm cloud's air currents are strong enough to keep lifting the hailstone back up into the growth area, and (3) if a hailstone is picked up by another cloud's air current and returned to its own growth area.

A hailstone finally falls to the ground when it gets too heavy for the air currents to support it, or when it is tossed to a new area with less uplifting air.

Just like other types of damaging storms, a hailstorm can be very dangerous to people and property. Some hailstones are large enough to break windows, damage roofs, and dent cars or other structures. In few cases, people and animals have been hurt or killed. Often though, hail is most damaging to crops that are ruined by the crushing and breaking of plants. Each year, hail causes costly damage to farmers.

Hail is most frequently seen by people found in Texas up through Alberta, Canada. The greatest amount of hail that falls in the United States hits southeastern Wyoming, western Nebraska, and eastern Colorado.

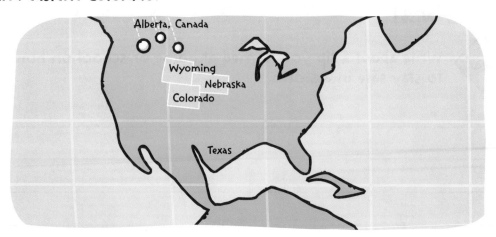

What Did the Story Say?

 Read Circle true or false for each sentence.

1. Hail cannot fall in the summer.	true	false
2. Hail only develops in very cold countries.	true	false
3. Hail can cause very costly damage.	true	false
4. Supercooled water exists in storm clouds.	true	false
5. Hail embryos start out big and get smaller.	true	false
6. Hailstones can get as big as baseballs.	true	false
7. Hails embryos are snow pellets.	true	false
8. A hailstone will only fall if it gets too heavy.	true	false
9. Air currents can carry hailstones to new clouds.	true	false
10. Hailstones are always smooth and round.	true	false

Weather Wise!

 Read Write about a tip you learned at home or school on how to stay safe in a storm.

_____

_____

_____

_____

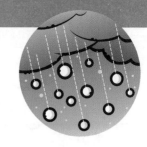

Word-Wise

Write the words from the story next to their meanings.

1. _____ frozen rain

2. _____ not common

3. _____ wet weather

4. _____ bump into

5. _____ something built

6. _____ expensive

precipitation

hail

collide

costly

rare

structure

Paying Attention to Details

List the three ways a hailstone can get larger.

1. _____

_____

2. _____

_____

3. _____

_____

21

There are some basic problems with staying underneath the water for any length of time. One problem is breathing, since a person needs air to stay alive. Another problem is water pressure — the weight of the water on a person's body. If you have ever picked up a gallon of water, you have felt its weight in your hands. Now imagine thousands of gallons of water over your head. You can see how quickly the pressure becomes unbearable as a person dives deeper.

Some of the first underwater divers used diving bells. These were made of thick, heavy metal or weighted barrels. A large bell was placed directly over the water and then lowered straight down until the bottom was reached. A small bell was placed on a person's head and then tied down securely. The top part of the bell remained filled with air. Early divers could not do much with these crude tools. They also had a very short time before their air supply was out and they needed to be lifted to the surface.

The idea of the undersea boat goes far back into history. With such a vessel, people could not only stay under the water, but they could move around to different locations.

Around 1620, a Dutch scientist named Cornelius van Drebbel showed his idea of an undersea rowboat in England. The design was covered in waterproof hides. Since then, other men invented different types of undersea boats, and by World War I submarines were being used to sink battleships.

On the surface, a modern submarine works very much like other large boats — but submarines spend very little time above water. The submarine is designed with an outer hull that is pressure proof. This keeps the crew and equipment from being crushed as the vessel dives deeper into the water. Also, tanks inside the hull fill with water to give the submarine ballast, or weight.

Once under the surface, the submarine has other special tools for getting around. An engine powers the propellers that drive the vessel and rudders help to steer it. Steel fins, called diving planes, help with diving, and a periscope can be used to see long distances (much like a telescope). A sail that is 20 feet high rises from the ship's deck and holds the periscope and radio equipment in place.

The modern submarine can stay underwater for months at a time. Some submarines have traveled underneath the ice at the North Pole and others all the way around the globe underwater.

So, the next time you eat a submarine sandwich, you might think about the amazing undersea vessel that it is named after.

What Did the Story Say?

 Read Write the answers.

1. What was the diving bell made of?

_____

2. Name two problems with staying underwater for a long time?

_____ and _____

3. When was the first undersea rowboat design shown in England?

_____

4. How was the submarine used in World War I?

_____

5. Why is the outer hull important to a submarine?

_____

_____

6. What makes the submarine able to dive and how does it work?

_____

_____

_____

7. Name three special tools that help the submarine get around.

_____

_____

8. How long can a modern submarine stay underwater?

_____

Word-Wise

 Read Draw a line from each word to the meaning used in the story.

securely	• used for steering
crude	• tightly
rudder	• simple
ballast	• engine-powered blades for moving forward
periscope	• weight
hide	• used for seeing long distances
propeller	• outer covering
hull	• animal skin

Design it!

 Read Design and draw your own submarine. Include the sail, propellers, and rudder.

While our home is the third planet from the sun, our neighbor Saturn is the sixth. It is second in size to Jupiter, which is the largest planet in the solar system.

Saturn is best known for its ring system and is mostly made of hydrogen gas. Toward the center of the planet, the hydrogen gas condenses into a liquid. Even closer to the center, the liquid hydrogen is compressed into metallic hydrogen. And finally at the center, there is thought to be a small, rocky core with a temperature near to 27,000° F. Now that's super hot!

Scientists have determined that a full rotation of the planet (one Saturn day) takes about 10 and a half hours. That's more than twice as fast as Earth's 24-hour rotation. Though the days may be much shorter than ours, it takes 29.6 Earth years for Saturn to make a complete orbit around the sun. That's about 10,804 days instead of 365 for Earth's smaller orbit.

Saturn's Rings

The rings of Saturn were first seen by Italian scientist Galileo in 1610. He was using one of the very first telescopes, so he thought that the rings were more like handles.

With better telescopes, the rings were later found to be separate from the planet and were labeled "A" through "E". Each ring is thought to consist of collections of rock, frozen gases, and ice. These objects can be as small as dust particles or as big as boulders.

Saturn's Moons

Saturn has 18 known moons. The planet may also have 14 new moons that have not been studied.

Most of Saturn's moons consist primarily of light, icy materials. Each moon has a name and a history of its own. Some are covered in craters and others are smoother.

Phoebe is the farthest moon from Saturn. It orbits in the opposite direction of the planet's other moons. Scientists suspect that Phoebe is probably a comet or part of one captured by Saturn's gravitational field.

Titan is the largest of Saturn's moons. Scientists believe it is larger than the planet Mercury. However, the exact size of Titan is not known because of a thick orange haze that hides its surface.

Visitors From Earth

The United States has sent many mechanical visitors into space. The Pioneer 11 probe flew by Saturn in 1979 and was followed by Voyager 1 in 1980 and Voyager 2 in 1981.

More recently, the National Aeronautics and Space Administration (NASA) sent the Cassini spacecraft toward Saturn in 1997. This spacecraft should reach Saturn in 2004.

Cassini is designed to study Saturn and its moons. It will even launch a probe, called the Huygens, into the atmosphere of the moon Titan. With Cassini, scientists are hoping to get better pictures and information about Saturn, its rings, and especially Titan.

What Did the Story Say?

Read Fill in the circle to finish the sentences.

1. Next to Jupiter, Saturn is the _____.
   ○ smallest planet in the solar system
   ○ roundest planet in the solar system
   ○ largest planet in the solar system

2. Saturn is mostly made of _____.
   ○ carbon dioxide gas
   ○ oxygen gas
   ○ hydrogen gas

3. One Saturn day equals _____.
   ○ 10 ½ hours
   ○ 24 hours
   ○ 29 hours

4. Saturn has _____ moons.
   ○ 14
   ○ 18
   ○ two

5. The rings of Saturn are thought to consist of _____.
   ○ rocks, dust, and light
   ○ rocks, frozen gases, and ice
   ○ lava, frozen gases, and ice

6. In 2004, the _____.
   ○ Voyager spacecraft is expected to return from Saturn
   ○ Cassini spacecraft is expected to arrive at Titan
   ○ Cassini spacecraft is expected to arrive at Saturn

Planet Neighbors

 Mark an X to show which planet is being described.

About the Planet	Saturn	Earth
I am the sixth planet from the sun.		
I have 18 moons.		
I am the third planet from the sun.		
I have a $10\frac{1}{2}$ hour day.		
There are 365 days in my year.		
My moon does not have a thick orange haze.		
My core is a small, hard, and rocky.		
One of my moons is larger than the planet Mercury.		
I am surrounded by rings.		
My NASA probes have been sent to visit far away places.		

Think About it!

 Pretend you are a space probe collecting information. Write some things you know about planet Earth.

_____

_____

The faster, the better — that's what I say. There's nothing I like more than going fast. When I'm gliding down the street with the wind rushing by, I feel so alive. The excitement of the rider helps to propel me. Oh, how I love being a bike.

A long time ago when Will was small, I had training wheels. That was the only time I remember going slowly. But it didn't take long for Will to get the hang of bike riding. He has great balance. Before long, he and I were taking long rides. And soon after, we were speeding alongside the older kids.

Once when I was still pretty new, Will's family took me and the other bikes camping with them. Will's dad bought a special rack for us to ride on the back of the camper. It was a long, bumpy ride, but we had such a fun time.

When we got to the camping grounds, we were all so excited that we could hardly keep quiet around the people. What hard work it was climbing up the mountain trails, but what joy we felt rolling back down. The other bikes and I can hardly wait until the next trip.

What makes me really happy is the first warm day in spring. That's when Will takes me out of the garage for my spring cleaning. He fills a bucket with warm, soapy water and rubs my frame until it shimmers. One spring, I even got a new coat of electric blue paint and some brand new safety reflectors. There's nothing more exhilarating than the first ride of the year!

What makes me sad is the first snow late in the fall. As soon as the snow comes, I get put away in the garage for many months. That's when I get a little jealous of the sleds. They are so sleek and shiny — perfect for racing down snowy hills. What fun it must be for a sled when it's snowy. I would like to sneak out just once and slide down a steep, snow-covered hill.

What makes me angry is a flat tire. Ouch! It hurts to run over a nail or glass. It is also kind of scary when my chain falls off. Will has to be very careful when that happens because the foot brakes don't work.

What makes me proud is how very careful Will is when he rides. He wears his bike helmet and follows the traffic rules. And he always pays attention. Even when we go really fast, I don't have to worry about Will doing anything dangerous and crashing me up. Like I said before, the faster, the better — but only if you're careful!

What Did the Story Say?

 Read Write the answers.

1. Who is telling the story? _____

2. Describe the one time when the bike went slowly.

_____

_____

3. What are some things that make the bike really happy?

_____

_____

_____

4. What makes the bike sad?

_____

_____

5. What makes the bike angry?

_____

6. What makes the bike proud?

_____

_____

_____

Real or Not?

Read Fill in the circle next to correct meaning.

1. propel
   - ○ pull back
   - ○ push forward
   - ○ stop

2. shimmer
   - ○ dry
   - ○ shake
   - ○ sparkle

3. exhilarating
   - ○ thrilling
   - ○ scary
   - ○ confusing

4. sleek
   - ○ smooth
   - ○ wet
   - ○ rough

The Author is You!

Read Imagine that you are a telephone. Write a short story about how you spend your day. Do you like being a telephone? Why?

_____

_____

_____

_____

_____

Amanda was fascinated with her Aunt's new poster hanging above the sofa. The poster was behind glass set in a polished gold frame. The people and animals were painted with bright colors and they looked old fashioned. Each person and building looked like it was perfectly placed in the country winter scene, almost like toys carefully laid out on the landscape.

"Aunt Kay," called Amanda, "who did this wonderful painting?"

"Grandma Moses," Aunt Kay replied. "She is my favorite American folk artist."

"Grandma Moses," laughed Amanda. "What a funny name for an artist. I never heard of her."

"She was a very interesting woman," said Aunt Kay. "Grandma Moses was born in New York in 1860, and she lived 101 years. Her real name was Anna Mary Robertson. I have her autobiography that she wrote when she was in her 90s. I'll show it to you."

Aunt Kay left the room and came back with the book. She and Amanda carefully leafed through it together.

"Why do they call her Grandma Moses?" Amanda asked.

"Well, most artists start painting at a very early age, but Grandma Moses was much older when she started," explained Aunt Kay. "You see, she enjoyed embroidery for a long time. But as she got older, her hands ached from arthritis and painting was less painful for her. By then she was already in her 70s. And she was almost 80 years old when she showed her first piece of artwork at the Museum of Modern Art in New York City in 1939."

"That is so cool!" exclaimed Amanda. "You hardly ever think of a grandparent like that. But you said she was a folk artist. What does that mean?"

"A folk artist paints, sculpts, or crafts things for the average person," continued Aunt Kay. "They make things for friends and families, not for museums or fancy art collectors. Like other folk artists, Grandma Moses never had any art lessons. Most of her paintings are based on her memories of her childhood in the late 1800s. They are kind of like pictures of the good old days."

"Well, I'm no fancy art collector," chuckled Amanda. "I think Grandma Moses is my favorite American folk artist, too!"

What Did the Story Say?

 Read Write the answers.

1. What is hanging above the sofa?

_____

2. Why is the painter called Grandma Moses?

_____

_____

3. Why does Aunt Kay know so much about Grandma Moses?

_____

_____

4. What is a folk artist?_____

_____

_____

5. What was Grandma Moses' real name?_____

6. What did Grandma Moses do before she started painting?

_____

7. What kinds of pictures did Grandma Moses paint?

_____

_____

8. What lesson do you think this story teaches?

_____

Interview with the Artist

Read Imagine that you are Grandma Moses and you are being interviewed by a newspaper reporter. Write your answers to the reporter's questions.

How did you get started in painting?

_____

_____

How would you describe your painting style?

_____

_____

Can you tell me about your first art show?

_____

_____

What can you tell me about the book you wrote?

_____

_____

About You

Read An autobiography is the story of a person's life that is written by that person. List four things you would want to include in your autobiography.

_____   _____

_____   _____

The timber wolf is a member of the gray wolf species within the dog family. Although it looks a lot like a German shepherd dog, it is bigger. The wolf's snout and legs are longer than a dog's.

The color of a wolf can vary, but it is usually gray. Most adult male wolves weigh between 75 and 120 pounds (34 to 54 kilograms). They have 42 teeth, including four fangs at the front of their mouths. These fangs can be up to two inches long.

The warm, bushy fur of a timber wolf allows its body to withstand cold climates, and its feet are large to help it walk on snow. Many timber wolves live in wooded habitats in northern areas like Alaska and Canada. There are also small numbers of wolves found in Minnesota, Michigan, Wisconsin, Montana, Idaho, and Washington.

Living in groups, or packs, of eight to 20, wolves are believed to have very strong feelings for each other. They also have a very clear social or ranking order within the pack. There are dominant members (the leaders) and subordinate members (the followers). All must follow strict rules for showing respect or rank.

The dominant male and female control where the pack stays, when it hunts, and how it raises the pups. When pack members meet, the dominant member stands up tall while the subordinate members crouch down. Once again, this is an indication of rank.

Each wolf pack lives in an area called a territory, which can cover between 30 and 800 square miles. Often attacking outsiders, the pack does not allow other wolves to hunt in its territory.

With superb eyesight, hearing, and sense of smell, the clever-minded wolf is an excellent hunter. The hunt begins with howling, which can get very loud as a way of warning outsider wolves to stay away.

Since many of the animals they hunt are bigger and faster, like caribou and elk, wolves have to be quick, too. Wolves will eat almost any animal they can catch, working as a team to finish the job.

Throughout history people have feared the wolf, even though they are known to keep away from people. They were often shown as the evil character in stories. They were thought to be a threat to farmers because they could kill sheep and cattle. And their ghostly sounding howls added to the fear.

In some areas of the world, wolves have been wiped out completely. However, in the United States, timber wolves have been reintroduced into the wild in Wyoming and Idaho, where they once roamed in great numbers.

What Did the Story Say?

Read Write the answers.

1. What type of habitat do timber wolves like? _____

_____

2. What animal is the timber wolf compared to in the story?

_____

3. Write three things that you learned about a wolf pack.

_____

_____

_____

4. Why do wolves howl?

_____

_____

5. Why are wolves excellent hunters? _____

_____

_____

6. Why do you think people have feared wolves in the past?

_____

_____

_____

What Did You Learn?

 Read Write the correct description for each category.

Timber Wolf
Hair (color and type):
Weight/size:
Similar looking animals:
Foot size: ____small ____medium ____large
Teeth:
Home state(s):
Other interesting facts:

Think About it!

Read You may have read or heard stories where the wolf is the bad or evil character. List a few of these stories below.

_____

_____

_____

_____

The sphinx is an important mythical creature. The word sphinx comes from the Greek language and was used to describe an imaginary evil monster. Throughout ancient times, the sphinx has appeared in many forms, such as huge stone statues, metal statues, pottery, paintings, and even as characters in mythical stories.

Most times, a sphinx was shown with the body of a lion and the face of a man or woman. Sometimes, it was shown with the head of a ram or a falcon. In Greece, there are many examples of sphinxes with a snake's tale and wings. In Egypt, statues of sphinxes were made to honor kings and queens. The king's or queen's face was used as a model for the head and the statue was believed to be a royal protector. Often, these statues were placed in tombs and burial grounds.

Oedipus's Sphinx

One very famous sphinx is not a statue but a character in Greek mythology. In the story of Oedipus, the sphinx lived on a high rock outside of Thebes and frightened the people of the city. She asked the same riddle to everyone who passed by: "What being has one voice and walks on four feet in the morning, two feet at noon, and then three feet in the evening?" If the passerby could not answer her riddle, she destroyed him or her.

One day, Oedipus passed by on his way to Thebes. When the sphinx asked him the riddle, Oedipus told her, "Man is the answer. He crawls on all fours as a baby, then walks on two legs, and then needs a cane in old age."

In the story, the sphinx was so angry that Oedipus had solved her riddle that she jumped from the rock to her death.

The Great Sphinx at Giza

In the dessert in Egypt stands the largest, oldest, and most famous sphinx statue, the Great Sphinx. This statue was built about 4,500 years ago and was mostly carved out of a giant limestone rock. The paws and legs were formed from cut stone blocks — the same stones that were used to build several of the great pyramids nearby.

Believed to be the protector of the pyramids, the Great Sphinx is 240 feet long and about 66 feet high. Its face measures 13 feet, 8 inches wide. Historians believe that the sphinx's face was modeled after King Khafre, whose tomb is nearby.

In the harsh dessert climate, the Great Sphinx has seen some hard times. It has been buried up to its neck several times in sand and had to be dug out. Also, its face is wearing away from the winds and blowing debris. Scientists are trying to protect this sphinx from further damage by treating it with special chemicals.

What Did the Story Say?

Read Fill in the blank to finish the sentence.

1. A sphinx is a _____ creature.

2. A sphinx has the body of a _____ and the
   _____ of a man or woman.

3. The story of Oedipus and the sphinx is a _____ myth.

4. The answer to the sphinx's riddle in the story of Oedipus is
   _____.

5. The_____ is a stone statue in Egypt.

6. Egyptians believe the sphinx was the _____ protector.

7. The Great Sphinx was mostly carved out of a _____ rock.

8. Because of the harsh dessert climate, the Great Sphinx has been
   _____ in sand and has had much wear on its
   _____ .

9. The same kinds of stones that make up the arms and legs of
   the sphinx were used to build several of the great
   _____ .

10. In Greek mythology, the riddling sphinx frightens the people
    in the city of _____ .

Word Search

Read Find and circle the words from the story. The words may go in any direction.

```
A  B  D  E  S  S  E  R  T  T  L
D  S  T  A  T  U  E  C  K  I  I
U  P  E  O  G  H  G  B  S  N  M
T  H  L  R  R  R  Y  S  M  P  E
P  I  D  O  E  V  E  N  D  O  S
Y  N  D  Y  S  I  T  E  N  P  T
G  X  I  A  K  P  I  L  K  A  O
E  R  R  L  D  E  B  R  I  S  N
T  H  E  B  E  S  L  I  O  N  E
```

sphinx	debris	Greek	tomb	Egypt	Thebes
limestone	royal	riddle	lion	dessert	statue

What's the Order?

Read According to the sphinx's riddle in the story of Oedipus, there are three stages of life. Write the number to put the stages in the correct order. Then draw a line to the time of day that goes with each stage.

Stage ☐ has three legs.　　　　　　　　morning

Stage ☐ has four legs.　　　　　　　　evening

Stage ☐ has two legs.　　　　　　　　noon

Speleology can be described as the study of cavities large enough for a person to stand in. So do speleologists study rotten dinosaur teeth? No. They study caves.

Any natural hollow space that is big enough to enter is considered a cave. Some caves end within a few steps, while others can stretch on for miles with many interconnecting passageways. The largest cave ever explored is the Mammoth-Flint Ridge Cave in Kentucky. This cave goes on for 340 miles, and scientists believe there is even more of it to be discovered.

Caves are formed in different ways. Some caves are formed over thousands of years as underground water wears away rock. Within that time, the earth may shift or the surroundings may change so the rock is exposed and most of the water drained away. What remains is known as a solution cave.

A lava tube cave is formed from hot flowing lava. What happens is the outer lava cools and hardens while the hot lava inside continues to flow. The hot lava finally drains from the tube to create a cave.

The third type of cave is a sea cave. These are formed from ocean waters as they erode the rocky shoreline.

Caves are usually dark, damp, and covered with strange formations called speleothems. Most of the eerie looking speleothems are made by trickling or seeping water. Of these formations, stalactites are the icicle-shaped spikes hanging down from the ceiling and stalagmites are the spikes that rise from the floor of the cave, or ground. A stalactite and a stalagmite can meet to form a column.

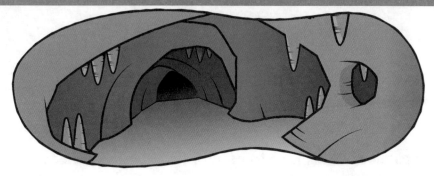

If you have trouble keeping stalactites and stalagmites straight, just remember that the one with the "g" (stalagmite) forms on the ground.

Even though they are dark and damp, caves have always been a good shelter for people. In some caves, prehistoric people drew artwork on the walls. These cave pictures show images of how they lived and survived in the times before written language and machinery.

Animals have also found shelter in caves. Bats are known to roost in caves during the day, flying out at night in large groups to hunt for insects. Other animals living in caves can include birds, rats, raccoons, and insects. And some bears use caves for a winter den.

But only very specialized animals called troglobites can live in the deepest, darkest part of caves where there is no light or wind. Such animals include certain fish, beetles, and spiders. Most troglobites are blind and have a thin or colorless skin or shell. They all have an excellent sense of smell and touch to make up for their lack of sight.

Hobbie Facts: If someone asks you to go spelunking, be sure to grab a helmet, a flashlight, some warm clothing, a pair of sturdy shoes, and some climbing gear because you are going cave exploring!

What Did the Story Say?

◇ **Read** ◇ Write the answers.

1. How big does a hole have to be in order to be considered a true cave?

_____

2. Where is the largest cave ever explored?_____

3. What are three animals that live in caves?

_____   _____   _____

4. What is it like inside a cave? How does it look and feel?

_____

5. Describe how a lava tube cave is formed.

_____

_____

6. What are two types of speleothems?

_____ and _____

7. Where do troglobites live?

_____

8. List four things that you would need to go spelunking?

_____   _____

_____   _____

A Trip Around Your Neighborhood!

Read Describe and draw three things you learned about caves from the story.

_____

_____

_____

- -

_____

_____

_____

- -

_____

_____

_____

Hobby Stuff

Read The story tells about the things needed for spelunking. Write the name of your favorite hobby and list four things you need to do it.

Your Hobby: _____

_____   _____

_____   _____

A picnic, a parade, a cookout, swimming, and the excitement of the new school year! These are all thoughts you may have when you think of Labor Day. But just like every other holiday, Labor Day has a special meaning behind it.

Labor Day was named in honor of working people throughout the United States, Puerto Rico, and Canada. It falls on the first Monday of September every year. Many businesses give their employees that day off, and many American families have traditions of enjoying the long weekend outdoors. Most consider Labor Day weekend the last "official" weekend of summer. In fact, Labor Day often marks the year's end for summertime activities such as swimming. Some outdoor ice cream shops in the colder areas of the country also close the day after Labor Day.

Europeans also celebrate Labor Day, but their holiday falls on May 1st. And other countries celebrate similar holidays to honor working people. Australia, for instance, celebrates Eight Hour Day to remember the struggles of a shorter working day.

In the United States, two men have been given the credit for the idea of having a holiday to honor working people. One was Matthew Maguire, a machinist from New Jersey. The other was Peter J. McGuire, a carpenter from New York City. These two men helped organize the very first Labor Day parade in New York City in September of 1882.

In 1887, Oregon was the first state to make Labor Day a legal holiday. Then President Grover Cleveland signed a bill in 1894, making it a national holiday.

How a Holiday Becomes "Legal"

In the United States, a legal holiday is an official day off work for all government employees. Our government allows each state to decide what days should be set aside as legal holidays. Each state's governor (the official elected leader of the state) proclaims the holidays and many businesses honor them as well. For all those who work for the federal government, the president and congress have declared the following as legal holidays:

* New Year's Day (January 1)
* Martin Luther King, Jr.'s, Birthday (January 15, but observed on the third Monday in January)
* Washington's Birthday (February 22, but observed on the third Monday in February)
* Memorial Day (the last Monday in May)
* Independence Day (July 4)
* Labor Day (the first Monday in September)
* Columbus Day (the second Monday in October)
* Veterans Day (November 11)
* Thanksgiving Day (the fourth Thursday in November)
* Christmas Day (December 25)

What Did the Story Say?

 Read   Write the answers.

1. Who does Labor Day honor? _____

2. Labor Day was named to honor people where?

_____ , _____ , and _____

3. Who is given credit in the United States for the idea of a

   holiday to honor working people?_____

   _____

   _____

4. Which state first declared Labor Day as a legal holiday?_____

5. List some labor day traditions mentioned in the story.

   _____   _____

   _____   _____

6. Who declares legal holidays in the federal government?

   _____ and _____

7. Who declares legal holidays for a state?

   _____

8. What do Australians call their holiday that honors
   working people?

   _____

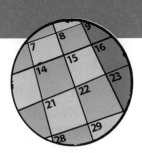

Happy Holiday

 Read Draw a line from the holiday to the correct month it is celebrated in.

Martin Luther King, Jr.'s, Birthday	• January
Memorial Day	• February
New Year's Day	• March
Washington's Birthday	• April
Independence Day	• May
Columbus Day	• June
Veterans Day	• July
Christmas Day	• August
Labor Day	• September
Thanksgiving Day	• October
	• November
	• December

Think About it!

 Read Does your family have any holiday traditions? Describe a holiday tradition that your family celebrates or make up one that you would like to start.

_____

_____

_____

Summer can sound like neighbors talking. It can sound like loud motorcycles and blaring sirens. It can also sound like the wind blowing through a maple tree, or a squirrel barking high up on a branch.

Sometimes I hear a blue jay's screech and the cicadas' call. A storm can creep up and surprise us all with loud booming thunder and pounding rain.

Summer can sound like friends laughing and kids shouting in the street. It can sound like a symphony of music and traffic.

And every summer night, the loud roar of the city is tamed into a muffled peace.

Summer can smell like hot tar on the street and dust on a windy day. It can smell like sweet barbecue sauce all up and down the street.

As the first drops hit the pavement, the smell of rain will fill the air. When the sun bakes the backyard, a delicious odor will rise from the tomato plants.

And don't forget the community pool. Nothing smells more refreshing than the pool water on a sweltering city day.

Oh, and the taste of summer — that's the best part! How can I forget the sweet taste of those juicy tomatoes? Is there anything more cooling than a big slice of juicy watermelon?

But then there's ice cream. In a cup, in a cone, in a bowl, on a stick, or straight from the carton, ice cream is summer!

The sights of summer are amazingly colorful. There are bright flowers in gardens and pots, and colorful laundry swinging in the air as it dries in the faint wind.

The summertime international festival is a feast for the eyes. There are bright flags, costumes, and fireworks that illuminate the night sky.

Summer feels good, too. It brings so many warm moments — and cool ones, too! Running through a sprinkler on a windy day can bring a chill. But lay down on your towel in the sunshine and that'll warm you right back up.

Summer can feel so hot on your back as you hike up the street to a friend's house at noon. It can feel like heat blazing down until you are sure your hair is going to catch fire. But summer can also be a warm, soothing breeze on your sweaty face after a late game of soccer, baseball, or kickball.

Heat, water, and wind are all wonderful feelings of summertime.

My friend, summer, has many faces that I am missing right now, as I sit here staring out at the backyard covered in snow. I can hardly wait for summer to visit me again.

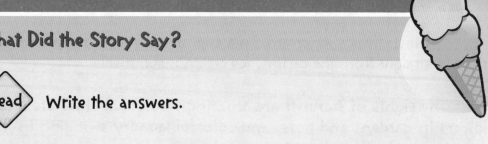

What Did the Story Say?

Read Write the answers.

1. Write three things that summer can sound like to the narrator of this story.

_____

_____

_____

2. The story takes place in the city. What images help you understand this point of view?

_____

_____

3. List some summer smells from the story.

_____

_____

_____

4. List some things that the narrator uses to describe how summer can feel.

_____

_____

_____

5. Describe the narrator's mood at the end of the story?

_____

_____

Word Meanings

Many words have more than one meaning. Fill in the circle next to the meaning from the story.

1. call
   - ○ to telephone a person
   - ○ to name something
   - ○ to cry out

2. delicious
   - ○ tasty
   - ○ pleasant
   - ○ flavorful

3. peace
   - ○ silence
   - ○ end of war
   - ○ stillness

4. chill
   - ○ relax
   - ○ refrigerate
   - ○ coolness

The Author is You!

Describe your favorite season using sound, smell, taste, feeling, and sight.

_____

_____

_____

_____

_____

_____

The Giant Squid

The giant squid has never been seen alive by human eyes, but scientists have studied many dead specimens.

Somewhere in the ocean, 900 to nearly 2,000 feet deep, the giant squid makes its home. This creature can weigh as much as 1,980 pounds (or 900 kilograms) and is the largest of all invertebrates (animals without a backbone). But the giant squid isn't just heavy, it's long, too. In fact, it is at least 60 feet (18 meters) long.

All squids are cephalopods, which means "head footed." Because the arms of the squid surround its mouth, you can see how it gets its name.

The squid breathes through gills and is designed to move quickly through the water. When it senses danger, it can eject an inky cloud to confuse its enemies. The inky cloud comes from a special body part called the ink gland.

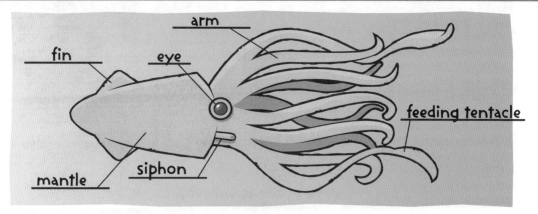

A squid has 10 arms. Eight of the arms are used to hold its food while it eats, and two extra long arms are used to catch the food. These long arms, or feeding tentacles, are lined with special hooks and suckers. A squid shoots them out quickly to grab food and bring it back toward its mouth. Then it uses its beak-like jaws to crush and tear the food

All squids have two eyes that are similar to human eyes. But a giant squid's eyes can be as big as volleyballs.

The mantle is the squid's main body part. It contains a kind of internal shell that helps to keep the squid's body stiff. Most squids use the mantle for swimming and two side fins for steering. By relaxing and tightening the mantle, the squid can swim forward, upward, and downward.

To move backward, the squid squirts water through a muscular funnel called the siphon. The siphon works like a jet engine to propel the animal backward.

Most squids are very quick in the water, but scientists are not sure about giant squids because they have never been seen swimming in their natural habitat. All smaller squids are food for many marine animals and humans, but giant squids are food for sperm whales.

What Did the Story Say?

 Read Circle true or false for each sentence.

1. Many giant squids have been seen in the deep ocean waters.	true false
2. A giant squid's eyes can be as big as volleyballs.	true false
3. The giant squid has an external shell.	true false
4. The siphon helps the squid swim.	true false
5. Scientists are not sure how fast giant squids swim.	true false
6. The giant squid is the largest invertebrate.	true false

Giant Squid Parts

 Read Label the picture.

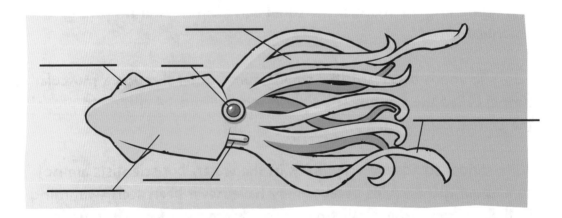

Puzzle Fun

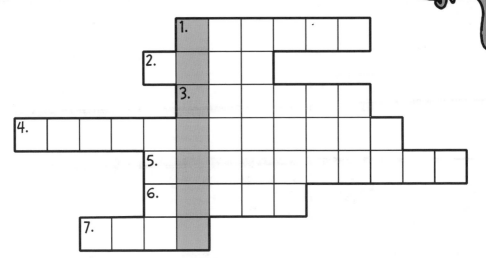

Read Use the clues to complete the puzzle.

1. The shell inside the giant squid's _____ helps to keep it stiff.

2. Giant squids have large human-like _____.

3. The _____ works kind of like a jet engine.

4. An animal with out a backbone is called an _____.

5. The scientific name for squid is _____.

6. A squid uses its beak-like jaws to _____ and tear its food.

7. A squid can release an _____ cloud to confuse its enemies.

Read Use the shaded letters to complete the sentence.

Giant squids will remain a kind of _____ until we are able to observe live ones in their ocean habitat.

Answer Key

How the Bear Lost his Tail
A Native American Tale

What Did the Story Say?

Read → Write the answers.

1. What was the bear so proud of?
his silky, long tail

2. How do the bear and the fox greet each other?
They call each other brother.

3. Why did the fox take the bear to the shallow part of the lake?
to trick him (he knew there were no fish there)

4. Besides placing his tail in the hole, what else did the fox tell the bear to do to catch a fish?
to clear his mind of all thoughts and concentrate

5. What was causing the ice to shake?
The bear was snoring loudly.

6. What was causing the fox to shake?
The fox was laughing hard.

7. Why do you think the bear listened to the fox? (Answers may vary.)
He was hungry for the fish. (or) He was silly.

8. Why do you think the bear pulled so hard? (Answers may vary.)
He was surprised. (or) He was scared.

9. What reasons does the bear have for moaning in the woods?
He misses his long tail and is still angry at the fox.

How the Bear Lost his Tail
A Native American Tale

What Happened Next?

Read → Number the sentences in the correct order to tell the story.

2 The fox sat with a circle of fat fish around him.

1 The fox decided to play a trick on the bear.

3 The fox took the bear to the shallow part of the lake.

4 The bear turned his back and stuck his tail in the fishing hole.

10 The bear has no love for the fox.

5 The fox went home to sleep in his cozy bed.

9 The bear chased the swift fox.

7 The fox shouted in the bear's ear.

8 The bear lost the part of his tail that was stuck to the ice.

6 The fox thought the bear looked like a small hill of snow.

Leaping Leprechauns

What Did the Story Say?

Read → Write the answers.

1. Describe the leprechaun that Cathleen saw.
He had pointy ears, a long, red beard, and wrinkles.

2. How did the leprechaun react when Cathleen surprised him?
He was angry. (or) He shook his fist at her.

3. Who warned Cathleen about how a leprechaun can trick people?
her grandmother

4. What does the leprechaun think about big people?
(Answers may vary.)   He thinks they are greedy.

5. Name three sounds Cathleen heard in the woods.
crickets, the hoot of an owl, the wind whistle,
and a loud rustling in the leaves

6. What mistake did Cathleen make that caused her to lose the pot of gold?
(Answers may vary.)
She looked away from the leprechaun.

7. Do you think Cathleen will have better luck the next time? Why?
(Answers may vary.)
No. The leprechaun is too tricky.

Leaping Leprechauns

Word Meanings

Read → Write the word next to its meaning.

1. recall — remember
2. clever — smart
3. fellow — man
4. wee — tiny
5. rustling — crackling
6. fury — anger
7. shrill — high-pitched
8. vanish — disappear

shrill
fellow
fury
recall
clever
wee
rustling
vanish

Think About it!

Read → How would you spend a whole pot of gold? Write your answer.

(Answers will vary.)

Captain James Cook the Explorer

What Did the Story Say?

Read → Circle the correct answer.

1. Captain James Cook was best know as a(n) ———.
a. explorer
b. cook
c. musician

2. Captain Cook's crew were the first to travel the coast of ———.
a. Africa and New Guinea
b. Australia and New Zealand
c. Austria and New Cumberland

3. Through his extensive travels, Captain Cook proved that all the ——— had been discovered.
a. countries
b. continents
c. oceans

4. Fewer sailors died on Captain Cook's explorations because he believed in ———.
a. making many stops
b. giving them clean clothes
c. feeding them fresh food

5. In his travels, Captain Cook discovered a group of islands he named the Sandwich Islands. These island were later renamed the ———.
a. Hawaiian Islands
b. Cook Islands
c. New Zealand Islands

6. When islanders got angry with Captain Cook's crew, it was because they ———.
a. bought too many souvenirs
b. brought too many pets on shore
c. took too much of the island food

Captain James Cook the Explorer

Puzzle Fun

Read → Use the clues to complete the puzzle.

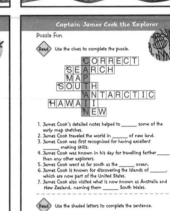

CORRECT
SEARCH
MAP
SOUTH
ANTARCTIC
HAWAII
NEW

1. James Cook's detailed notes helped to _____ some of the early map sketches.
2. James Cook traveled the world in _____ of new land.
3. James Cook was first recognized for having excellent _____ making skills.
4. James Cook was known in his day for travelling farther _____ than any other explorers.
5. James Cook went as far south as the _____ ocean.
6. James Cook is known for discovering the islands of _____, which are now part of the United States.
7. James Cook also visited what is now known as Australia and New Zealand, naming them _____ South Wales.

Read → Use the shaded letters to complete the sentence.

James Cook was a very impressive sea **CAPTAIN** who made many discoveries in the mid 1700s.

An Amazing Ride

What Did the Story Say?

Read → Fill in the blank to finish the sentence.

1. Maddie really wanted to ride on the **Ferris wheel**.

2. The large basket attached to a hot air balloon is called the **gondola**.

3. There was a strange, loud **crackling** sound right before the balloon started drifting away.

4. A person can throw out the **ballast** to decrease the weight being lifted by the balloon.

5. Maddie's mom fired up the **burner** to get the balloon to rise.

6. Maddie and her mom heard **cheering** when they landed on top of the Ferris wheel.

Think About it!

Read → At the end of the story, the characters land on top of the Ferris wheel. How do you imagine they got down to the ground? Write your answer.

(Answers will vary.)
They rode the Ferris wheel to the ground.

An Amazing Ride

A Trip Around Your Neighborhood!

Read → Write a short story about a balloon trip you would take over your neighborhood. Then draw a picture that goes with your story.

(Answers will vary.)

(Drawings will vary.)

All Hail the Hail!

What Did the Story Say?

Read → Circle true or false for each sentence.

1. Hail cannot fall in the summer. true **false**
2. Hail only develops in very cold countries. true **false**
3. Hail can cause very costly damage. **true** false
4. Supercooled water exists in storm clouds. **true** false
5. Hail embryos start out big and get smaller. true **false**
6. Hailstones can get as big as baseballs. **true** false
7. Hails embryos are snow pellets. **true** false
8. A hailstone will only fall if it gets too heavy. **true** false
9. Air currents can carry hailstones to new clouds. **true** false
10. Hailstones are always smooth and round. true **false**

Weather Wise!

Read → Write about a tip you learned at home or school on how to stay safe in a storm.

(Answers will vary.) If there is a tornado
warning and you are at home, go down to the
basement or inside the closet on the first floor
that is closest to the middle of the house.

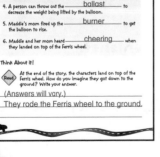

62

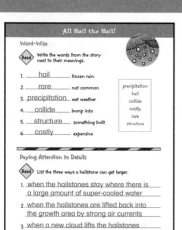

All Hail the Hail!

Word-Wise

Read Write the words from the story next to their meanings.

1. __hail__ frozen rain
2. __rare__ not common
3. __precipitation__ wet weather
4. __collide__ bump into
5. __structure__ something built
6. __costly__ expensive

Word box: precipitation, hail, collide, costly, rare, structure

Paying Attention to Details

Read List the three ways a hailstone can get larger.

1. when the hailstones stay where there is a large amount of super-cooled water
2. when the hailstones are lifted back into the growth area by strong air currents
3. when a new cloud lifts the hailstones into its growth area

21

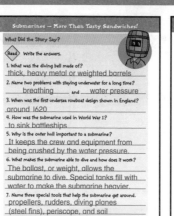

Submarines — More Than Tasty Sandwiches!

What Did the Story Say?

Read Write the answers.

1. What was the diving bell made of?
thick, heavy metal or weighted barrels
2. Name two problems with staying underwater for a long time?
breathing and water pressure
3. When was the first undersea rowboat design shown in England?
around 1620
4. How was the submarine used in World War I?
to sink battleships
5. Why is the outer hull important to a submarine?
It keeps the crew and equipment from being crushed by the water pressure.
6. What makes the submarine able to dive and how does it work?
The ballast, or weight, allows the submarine to dive. Special tanks fill with water to make the submarine heavier.
7. Name three special tools that help the submarine get around.
propellers, rudders, diving planes (steel fins), periscope, and sail
8. How long can a modern submarine stay underwater?
for months at a time

24

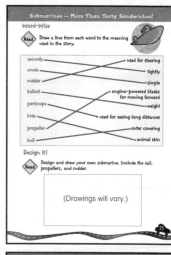

Submarines — More Than Tasty Sandwiches!

Word-Wise

Read Draw a line from each word to the meaning used in the story.

securely — tightly
crude — simple
rudder — used for steering
ballast — weight
periscope — engine-powered blades for moving forward
hide — used for seeing long distances
propeller — animal skin
hull — outer covering

Design it!

Read Design and draw your own submarine. Include the sail, propellers, and rudder.

(Drawings will vary.)

25

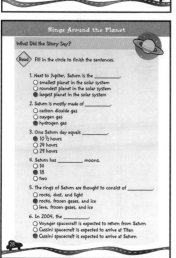

Rings Around the Planet

What Did the Story Say?

Read Fill in the circle to finish the sentences.

1. Next to Jupiter, Saturn is the _____.
  ○ smallest planet in the solar system
  ○ roundest planet in the solar system
  ● largest planet in the solar system
2. Saturn is mostly made of _____.
  ○ carbon dioxide gas
  ○ oxygen gas
  ● hydrogen gas
3. One Saturn day equals _____.
  ● 10 ½ hours
  ○ 24 hours
  ○ 29 hours
4. Saturn has _____ moons.
  ○ 14
  ● 18
  ○ two
5. The rings of Saturn are thought to consist of _____.
  ○ rocks, dust, and light
  ● rocks, frozen gases, and ice
  ○ lava, frozen gases, and ice
6. In 2004, the _____.
  ○ Voyager spacecraft is expected to return from Saturn
  ○ Cassini spacecraft is expected to arrive at Titan
  ● Cassini spacecraft is expected to arrive at Saturn

28

Rings Around the Planet

Planet Neighbors

Read Mark an X to show which planet is being described.

About the Planet	Saturn	Earth
I am the sixth planet from the sun.	X	
I have 18 moons.	X	
I am the third planet from the sun.		X
I have a 10 ½ hour day.	X	
There are 365 days in my year.		X
My moon does not have a thick orange haze.		X
My core is a small, hard, and rocky.		X
One of my moons is larger than the planet Mercury.	X	
I am surrounded by rings.	X	
My NASA probes have been sent to visit far away places.	X	

Think About It!

Read Pretend you are a space probe collecting information. Write some things you know about planet Earth.

(Answers will vary.)

29

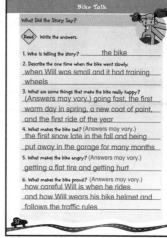

Bike Talk

What Did the Story Say?

Read Write the answers.

1. Who is telling the story? __the bike__
2. Describe the one time when the bike went slowly.
when Will was small and it had training wheels
3. What are some things that make the bike really happy?
(Answers may vary.) going fast, the first warm day in spring, a new coat of paint, and the first ride of the year
4. What makes the bike sad? (Answers may vary.)
the first snow late in the fall and being put away in the garage for many months
5. What makes the bike angry? (Answers may vary.)
getting a flat tire and getting hurt
6. What makes the bike proud? (Answers may vary.)
how careful Will is when he rides and how Will wears his bike helmet and follows the traffic rules

32

Bike Talk

Real or Not?

Read Fill in the circle next to correct meaning.

1. propel
  ○ pull back
  ● push forward
  ○ stop
2. shimmer
  ○ dry
  ○ shake
  ● sparkle
3. exhilarating
  ● thrilling
  ○ scary
  ○ confusing
4. sleek
  ● smooth
  ○ wet
  ○ rough

The Author is You!

Read Imagine that you are a telephone. Write a short story about how you spend your day. Do you like being a telephone? Why?

(Stories will vary.)

33

Grandma Moses

What Did the Story Say?

Read Write the answers.

1. What is hanging above the sofa? (Answers may vary.)
Aunt Kay's new poster (or) a painting by Grandma Moses
2. Why is the painter called Grandma Moses? (Answers may vary.)
She was much older than most artists were when she started painting. (or) She was in her 70s when she started painting.
3. Why does Aunt Kay know so much about Grandma Moses?
(Answers may vary.) Grandma Moses is her favorite folk artist. (or) She has Grandma Moses' autobiography.
4. What is a folk artist? __(Answers may vary.)__
an artist who paints, sculpts, or crafts things for the average person (or) an artist who never had any art lessons
5. What was Grandma Moses' real name? Anna Mary Robertson
6. What did Grandma Moses do before she started painting?
She liked to do embroidery.
7. What kinds of pictures did Grandma Moses paint?
(Answers may vary.) She painted pictures based on memories of her childhood. (or) She painted old-fashioned country scenes.
8. What lesson do you think this story teaches? (Answers may vary.)
You are never too old to learn something new.

36

Grandma Moses

Interview with the Artist

Read Imagine that you are Grandma Moses and you are being interviewed by a newspaper reporter. Write your answers to the reporter's questions.
(Answers may vary.)

How did you get started in painting?
I always liked to embroider, but my arthritis made it hard. So I started painting.
How would you describe your painting style?
I like to paint what I remember from my childhood. My style is folk art.
Can you tell me about your first art show?
I had my first show in New York City. It was 1939 and I was almost 80 years old then.
What can you tell me about the book you wrote?
I wrote my autobiography. It tells about my life and my art. I wrote this book when I was in my 90s.

About You

Read An autobiography is the story of a person's life that is written by that person. List four things you would want to include in your autobiography.

(Answers will vary.)

37

63

Answer Key

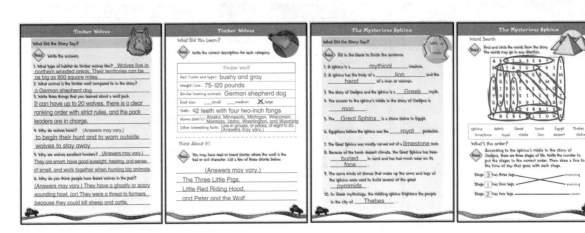

Timber Wolves

What Did the Story Say?

Read) Write the answers.

1. What type of habitat do timber wolves like? Wolves live in northern wooded areas. Their territories can be as big as 800 square miles.

2. What animal is the timber wolf compared to in the story? a German shepherd dog

3. Write three things that you learned about a wolf pack. It can have up to 20 wolves, there is a clear ranking order with strict rules, and the pack leaders are in charge.

4. Why do wolves howl? (Answers may vary.) to begin their hunt and to warn outside wolves to stay away

5. Why are wolves excellent hunters? (Answers may vary.) They are smart, have good eyesight, hearing, and sense of smell, and work together when hunting big animals.

6. Why do you think people have feared wolves in the past? (Answers may vary.) They have a ghostly or scary sounding howl. (or) They were a threat to farmers because they could kill sheep and cattle.

Timber Wolves

What Did You Learn?

Read) Write the correct description for each category.

Timber Wolf

Hair (color and type): bushy and gray

Weight/size: 75-120 pounds

Similar looking animals: German shepherd dog

Foot size: ___ small ___ medium ✗ large

Teeth: 42 teeth with four two-inch fangs

Home state(s): Alaska, Minnesota, Michigan, Wisconsin, Montana, Idaho, Washington, and Wyoming

Other interesting facts: Live in groups, or packs, of eight to 20. (Answers may vary.)

Think About It!

Read) You may have read or heard stories where the wolf is the bad or evil character. List a few of these stories below.

(Answers may vary.)
The Three Little Pigs,
Little Red Riding Hood,
and Peter and the Wolf.

The Mysterious Sphinx

What Did the Story Say?

Read) Fill in the blank to finish the sentence.

1. A sphinx is a ___mythical___ creature.

2. A sphinx has the body of a ___lion___ and the head ___ of a man or woman.

3. The story of Oedipus and the sphinx is a ___Greek___ myth.

4. The answer to the sphinx's riddle in the story of Oedipus is ___man___.

5. The ___Great Sphinx___ is a stone statue in Egypt.

6. Egyptians believe the sphinx was the ___royal___ protector.

7. The Great Sphinx was mostly carved out of ___limestone___ rock.

8. Because of the harsh desert climate, the Great Sphinx has been ___buried___ in sand and has had much wear on its ___face___.

9. The same kinds of stones that make up the arms and legs of the sphinx were used to build several of the great ___pyramids___.

10. In Greek mythology, the riddling sphinx frightens the people in the city of ___Thebes___.

The Mysterious Sphinx

Word Search

Read) Find and circle the words from the story. The words may go in any direction.

[word search grid]

sphinx   debris   Greek   tomb   Egypt   Thebes
limestone   royal   riddle   lion   dessert   statue

What's the order?

Read) According to the sphinx's riddle in the story of Oedipus, there are three stages of life. Write the number to put the stages in the correct order. Then draw a line to the time of day that goes with each stage.

Stage [3] has three legs. ———— morning
Stage [1] has four legs. ———— evening
Stage [2] has two legs. ———— noon

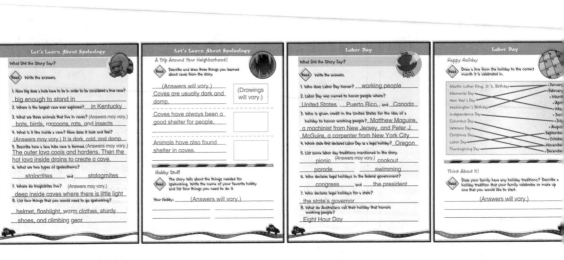

Let's Learn About Speleology

What Did the Story Say?

Read) Write the answers.

1. How big does a hole have to be in order to be considered a true cave? big enough to stand in

2. Where is the largest cave ever explored? in Kentucky

3. What are three animals that live in caves? (Answers may vary.) bats, birds, raccoons, rats, and insects

4. What is it like inside a cave? How does it look and feel? (Answers may vary.) It is dark, cold, and damp.

5. Describe how a lava tube cave is formed. (Answers may vary.) The outer lava cools and hardens. Then the hot lava drains to create a cave.

6. What are two types of speleothems? ___stalactites___ and ___stalagmites___

7. Where do troglobites live? (Answers may vary.) deep inside caves where there is little light

8. List four things that you would need to go spelunking? helmet, flashlight, warm clothes, sturdy shoes, and climbing gear

Let's Learn About Speleology

A Trip Around Your Neighborhood!

Read) Describe and draw three things you learned about caves from the story.

(Answers will vary.)
Caves are usually dark and damp.

(Drawings will vary.)

Caves have always been a good shelter for people.

Animals have also found shelter in caves.

Hobby Stuff

Read) The story tells about the things needed for spelunking. Write the name of your favorite hobby and list four things you need to do it.

Your Hobby: (Answers will vary.)

Labor Day

What Did the Story Say?

Read) Write the answers.

1. Who does Labor Day honor? working people

2. Labor Day was named to honor people where? United States, Puerto Rico, and Canada

3. Who is given credit in the United States for the idea of a holiday to honor working people? Matthew Maguire, a machinist from New Jersey, and Peter J. McGuire, a carpenter from New York City

4. Which state first declared Labor Day as a legal holiday? Oregon

5. List some labor day traditions mentioned in the story. (Answers may vary.) picnic   cookout   parade   swimming

6. Who declares legal holidays in the federal government? congress and the president

7. Who declares legal holidays for a state? the state's governor

8. What do Australians call their holiday that honors working people? Eight Hour Day

Labor Day

Happy Holiday

Read) Draw a line from the holiday to the correct month it is celebrated in.

Martin Luther King, Jr.'s Birthday ——— January
Memorial Day ——— February
New Year's Day ——— March
Washington's Birthday ——— April
Independence Day ——— May
Columbus Day ——— June
Veterans Day ——— July
Christmas Day ——— August
Labor Day ——— September
Thanksgiving Day ——— October
——— November
——— December

Think About It!

Read) Does your family have any holiday traditions? Describe a holiday tradition that your family celebrates or make up one that you would like to start.

(Answers will vary.)

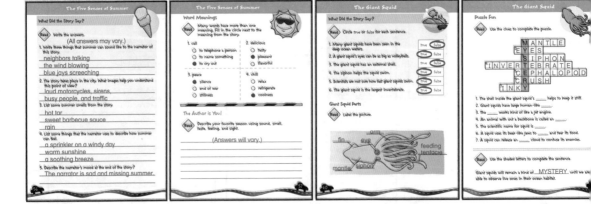

The Five Senses of Summer

What Did the Story Say?

Read) Write the answers.

(All answers may vary.)

1. Write three things that summer can sound like to the narrator of this story. neighbors talking   the wind blowing   blue jays screeching

2. The story takes place in the city. What images help you understand this point of view? loud motorcycles, sirens, busy people, and traffic

3. List some summer smells from the story. hot tar   sweet barbecue sauce   rain

4. List some things that the narrator uses to describe how summer can feel. a sprinkler on a windy day   warm sunshine   a soothing breeze

5. Describe the narrator's mood at the end of the story? The narrator is sad and missing summer.

The Five Senses of Summer

Word Meanings

Read) Many words have more than one meaning. Fill in the circle next to the meaning from the story.

1. call
○ to telephone a person
○ to name something
● to cry out

2. delicious
○ tasty
● pleasant
○ flavorful

3. peace
● silence
○ end of war
○ stillness

4. chill
○ relax
○ refrigerate
● coolness

The Author Is You!

Read) Describe your favorite season using sound, smell, taste, feeling, and sight.

(Answers will vary.)

The Giant Squid

What Did the Story Say?

Read) Circle true or false for each sentence.

1. Many giant squids have been seen in the deep ocean waters. true (false)

2. A giant squid's eyes can be as big as volleyballs. (true) false

3. The giant squid has an external shell. true (false)

4. The siphon helps the squid swim. (true) false

5. Scientists are not sure how fast giant squids swim. (true) false

6. The giant squid is the largest invertebrate. (true) false

Giant Squid Parts

Read) Label the picture.

arm
fin   eye   feeding tentacle
mantle   siphon

The Giant Squid

Puzzle Fun

Read) Use the clues to complete the puzzle.

MANTLE
EYES
SIPHON
INVERTEBRATE
CEPHALOPOD
CRUSH
INKY

1. The shell inside the giant squid's ___ helps to keep it stiff.
2. Giant squids have large human-like ___.
3. The ___ works kind of like a jet engine.
4. An animal with out a backbone is called an ___.
5. The scientific name for squid is ___.
6. A squid uses its beak-like jaws to ___ and tear its food.
7. A squid can release an ___ cloud to confuse its enemies.

Read) Use the shaded letters to complete the sentence.

Giant squids will remain a kind of ___MYSTERY___ until we are able to observe live ones in their ocean habitat.